# El asombroso, estupendo, extraordinario y algo inusual
# LIBRO GIRATORIO

No necesita pilas

# The Amazing, Stupendous, Extraordinary, and Somewhat Unusual
# SPINNING BOOK

No Batteries Required

Jimmy Huston

Copyright © 2019-24 Jimmy Huston

ISBN 978-1-965153-03-1

Todos los derechos reservados, incluido el derecho a usar o reproducir este libro o cualquiera de sus partes sin el consentimiento escrito de la editorial a excepción de cuando se trate de citas breves contenidas dentro de críticas o reseñas.

All rights reserved, including the right to use or reproduce this book or portions thereof in any form whatsoever without written permission from the publisher except in the case of brief quotations embodied in critical articles or reviews.

Cosworth Publishing
21545 Yucatan Avenue
Woodland Hills, CA 91364
*www.cosworthpublishing.com*

Para más información sobre este consentimiento, escríbanos a *office@cosworthpublishing.com*.

For information regarding permission, please send an email to *office@cosworthpublishing.com*

*Dedicado a la lectura peligrosa.*
*Dedicated to reading dangerously.*

# Índice de contenidos

PARTE I...........................................1

PARTE II.........................................37

# Table of Contents

PART I............................................1

PART II..........................................37

# PARTE I

## Capítulo Uno

# PART I

## Chapter One

¿Nada?

Nothing?

¿Eh...?

Huh...?

¿Y ahora?

What about now?

Intenta hacer un sonido con la boca.

Try making a sound with your mouth.

Tal vez un ruido de motor chisporroteando o un trompo zumbando...

Maybe a sputtering engine noise or a whirring spinning top...

¿Todavía nada?


Still nothing?

Sigue probando. Tal vez un ruido diferente.

Keep trying. Maybe a different noise.

¡Ajá! ¡Eso funciona!

Aha! That works!

Sigue intentándolo. ¡Puedes hacerlo!

Keep going. You can do it!

¿Qué ha pasado?

What happened?

¿Dejaste de hacer ruido?
Inténtalo de nuevo.

Did you stop making noise?
Try again.

¡Eso es! ¡Sigue así!

That's it! Keep it going!

Le estás cogiendo el truco.

You're getting the hang of it.

Pero no puedes estar enderezando el libro.

But you can't be straightening the book.

Tienes que seguir. Inténtalo otra vez.

You've got to keep it going. Try again.

No. ¿Estás haciendo ruido?

Nope. Are you making the noise?

Más alto. ¡A por ello!

Louder. Go for it!

¡Sí! ¡Eso funciona!

Yes! That's working!

That's it! Keep it going!

¡Eso es! ¡Adelante!

Cuando pases la página,
When you turn the page,

feed the book through your fingers.

alimenta el libro a través de tus dedos.

¡Sí, lo estás haciendo. ¡No pares!
Yes, you're doing it. Don't stop!

Lo has hecho antes, ¿verdad?

You've done this before, haven't you?

Ahora acelera. Lee más rápido.
Now speed it up. Read faster.

Después de todo… la gente está mirando.
After all -- people are watching.

¿Es tan rápido como puedes leer?
¿De verdad?

Is that as fast as you can read? Really?

Y deja de mover los labios.

And stop moving your lips.

Cuando seas realmente bueno --

When you get really good --

-- podrás hacer esto con tus libros de texto.

-- you can do this with your textbooks.

Pero aún no eres tan bueno.

But you're not that good yet.

Vale... ¡PARA! Pero no te relajes.

Okay -- STOP! But don't relax.

Ahora vamos en la otra dirección.

Now we're going in the other direction.

Uy. Sabes lo que esto significa.

Oops. You know what this means.

No estás haciendo tus ruidos. ¡Vamos!

You're not making your noises. Go!

Así. ¡Así se hace!

That's it. Way to go!

Yikes. This way is harder.

Yikes. Este camino es más difícil.

*No te hagas daño. ¡¡¡Weeeeeeeeee!!!*

*Don't hurt yourself. Wheeeeeeee!!!*

¿Estás seguro de que no puedes leer más rápido?

Entonces sáltate las palabras y pasa la página.

Are you sure you can't read any faster?

Then skip the words and just turn the page.

Al final, habrá una prueba.

At the end, there's going to be a test.

Y recuerda. Hagas lo que hagas --
And remember. Whatever you do --

-- NO pienses en marearte.
-- do NOT think about being dizzy.

Puede ser muy divertido enseñar este libro a los mayores.

It can be lots of fun to show this book to grownups.

Uf. Tómate un descanso.
Recupera el aliento.

Whew. Take a break.
Catch your breath.

# PARTE II

# Capítulo dos

# PART II

# Chapter Two

# El final

# The End

## Sobre el autor

Está demasiado mareado para terminar...

## About the Author

He's too dizzy to finish...

**Otros libros de Jimmy Huston**

**Also by Jimmy Huston**

*The I Hate to Read Book*

*...and I Hate Math 2*

*Nate-Nate the Christmas Snake*

*The Dyslexic Handbook: Genius Edition*

*Cussing for Kids!: Etiquette for the Profane*

*The Attention Deficit Disorder Hyperactive Cookbook: Puzzle Edition*

*Autism for Beginners: Surfing the Spectrum*

*The OCD Funbook: Really?*

*The Bedtime Book of Bad Dreams: Dozing Dangerously*

*Baby's First Instruction Manual: How To Be the Center of the Universe*

*Rat BLEEP and Alien Poop: Not for Parents at All*

*The Big Beautiful Book of Burping, Belching, and Barfing*

*The Book Book: Inside the Inside Story*

*Why Can't Mommy Spend More Time with Me?*

*How to Write This Book: You're Going To Be the Author*

*That Damn Little Angel*

*The Snake Test: True? False? Maybe?*

*Is This Your First Funeral?: A Child's Primer*

*The First Apology Is the Worst*

*Don't Go to College, Go to Europe for Less*

*Dead Is the New Sick: An Insider's Guide to Senility, Paranoia, and Curmudgery*

*www.byjimmyhuston.com*
*www.cosworthpublishing.com*

www.ingramcontent.com/pod-product-compliance
Lightning Source LLC
LaVergne TN
LVHW070207080526
838202LV00063B/6571